DiscoverRoo
n Imprint of Pop!
obooksonline.com

HAUNTED HOMES

by Elizabeth Andrews

abdobooks.com

Published by Pop!, a division of ABDO, PO Box 398166, Minneapolis, Minnesota 55439. Copyright © 2022 by Abdo Consulting Group, Inc. International copyrights reserved in all countries. No part of this book may be reproduced in any form without written permission from the publisher. DiscoverRoo™ is a trademark and logo of Pop!.

Printed in the United States of America, North Mankato, Minnesota.

102021
012022

Cover Photos: Shutterstock Images (photo and pattern)

Interior Photos: Shutterstock Images, 1, 5, 6, 9, 13, 14, 17, 18–19, 20, 25, 26, 29; Universal History Archive/UIG/Shutterstock, 10

Editor: Tyler Gieseke
Series Designer: Laura Graphenteen

Library of Congress Control Number: 2021943409
Publisher's Cataloging-in-Publication Data

Names: Andrews, Elizabeth, author.

Title: Haunted homes / by Elizabeth Andrews

Description: Minneapolis, Minnesota : Pop!, 2022 | Series: Hauntings | Includes online resources and index.

Identifiers: ISBN 9781098241230 (lib. bdg.) | ISBN 9781644946763 (pbk.) | ISBN 9781098241933 (ebook)

Subjects: LCSH: Haunted places--Juvenile literature. | Ghosts --Juvenile literature. | Haunted houses--Juvenile literature. | Ghost Stories--Juvenile literature.

Classification: DDC 133.12--dc23

WELCOME TO DiscoverRoo!

Pop open this book and you'll find QR codes loaded with information, so you can learn even more!

Scan this code* and others like it while you read, or visit the website below to make this book pop!

popbooksonline.com/haunted-homes

*Scanning QR codes requires a web-enabled smart device with a QR code reader app and a camera.

TABLE OF
CONTENTS

CHAPTER 1

ENTER AT YOUR OWN RISK

Haunted houses are a Halloween classic.

Almost everyone enjoys getting a good

scare, especially when they know the

zombie waiting in the shadows is just a

teenager in costume. And the hot apple

WATCH A VIDEO HERE!

Haunted houses are especially popular during the Halloween season.

cider handed out before the hayride can soothe anyone's nerves when things get a little too spooky.

Ghosts can show up in many different ways. Some take on their former human shapes.

But what about the homes that are

haunted by *real* ghosts instead of people

in costumes? How do you remain calm

when a strange voice drifts down a

dark staircase?

When tragedy strikes, it can stir

up strong emotions. These emotions

are often what ties a spirit to a place.

Homes can be the setting for the

biggest joys of people's lives. They can

also hold moments of anger, hurt, pain,

and sadness. It's scary to think that a

warm home can become so cold and

frightening. But sometimes, that's exactly

what happens.

CHAPTER 2

TORTURE HOUSE

A woman named Madame Marie

Delphine LaLaurie lived in a New Orleans,

Louisiana, mansion. She was awful

most of her life. It was said that her

LEARN MORE
HERE!

Enslavers would use chains to prevent their captives from getting free.

third marriage sent her into madness.

Marie was known for being cruel to her

daughters and the people she enslaved.

Marie's wickedness was clear

after a fire at the mansion in 1834. It

was said that the cook, who Marie had

Madame LaLaurie would punish her daughters if she caught them giving food to the people she enslaved.

chained to the stove, started it. During the blaze, firefighters heard wails and screams coming from the attic. When they broke the door down, they found a **torture chamber**.

The enslaved people at the LaLaurie home were chained to the walls, strapped to surgery carts, and locked in cages. They had been experimented on and beaten. Some were dead and some were barely alive. The madame and her family fled during the fire. No one ever saw them again.

Marie's evil remained in the mansion though. Through new owners, new walls, and new centuries, the voices of those tortured by Madame LaLaurie can still be heard. Cries of pain, slamming doors, and moving furniture are constant. Shadowed figures of people hunched over from chains around their necks roam the attic.

DID YOU KNOW? New Orleans, Louisiana, has more than 300 years of spooky history. There are a few nighttime ghost tours for visitors to choose from.

Most of the LaLaurie Mansion had to be rebuilt after the fire.

People have seen a young girl jump from the balcony as if she was being chased by someone or something awful.

At some point, the mansion was turned into apartments. One mother who lived there said she witnessed a woman dressed in black throw the mother's twin babies down the stairs. After quickly running to their room, she found the babies still asleep in their crib. When the mother checked on the children the next night, she saw the same woman in black hovering over them as they slept.

People often see ghosts dressed in long robes.

As time passes, the hauntings in the mansion continue. A new owner decided to make repairs. He found graves beneath the old floors. It is thought that Madame LaLaurie had hidden the bodies of the enslaved people who died there. The LaLaurie mansion will likely hold on to those haunted souls forever.

CHAPTER 3
NOT MUCH OF A VACATION HOME

In the Philippines, the Laperal White House

sits in a lovely vacation town called

Baguio. It was built in the 1930s for the

Laperal family. Don Roberto led the family.

He built his home in Southeast Asia in

COMPLETE AN ACTIVITY HERE!

the American Colonial style. The house is

large and white. It stands out among the

thick trees and plants surrounding it.

Don Roberto's wife loved taking care of the plants around their white house.

Roberto and his wife chose Baguio

for their summer home because it

offered a break from their everyday

lives. Unfortunately, the new house did

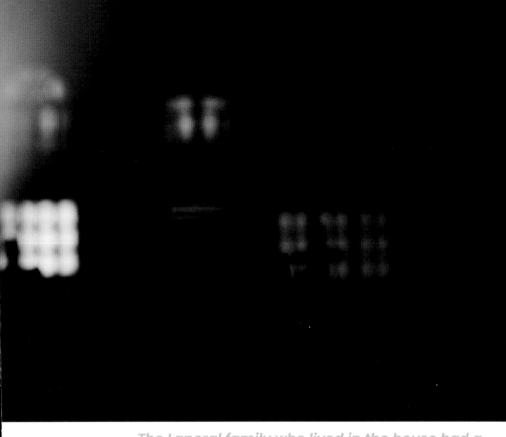

The Laperal family who lived in the house had a father, mother, young daughter, and a nanny.

not bring the Laperal family the peace

they were looking for. In fact, it seemed

to curse most people who stepped

foot inside.

Many times, ghosts appear in the exact place they died.

Tragedy first struck at the white house when the Laperals' three-year-old daughter wandered away from her nanny and into the street out front. She was hit by a car and died. The nanny felt so guilty that she soon took her own life in the attic.

It is said that the little girl haunts the front steps. People have seen her standing on the third step, just watching people as they pass by. The ghost of the nanny can be seen in the attic window. People say she never takes her eyes off the ghost of the Laperals' little girl. Perhaps they are bound together forever.

WARTIME

During **World War II**, the Philippines were taken over by the Japanese. Any home could be stolen from its owners. The Japanese soldiers turned homes into **garrisons**. This included the Laperal home. Anyone the Japanese suspected of working for the enemy would be jailed. Prisoners were **tortured** and killed. Many who pass the white house say they hear the cries of the people who died.

The Laperals couldn't stay in the house during World War II. But when the war ended, Roberto returned to the home. By this time, he had lost his wife and all their children. He was alone. The vacation house did not feel the same after that, so he decided to leave it to relatives.

When he walked down the haunted front steps for the last time, he slipped and fell. The fall killed him. His ghost has never left. It is seen going up and down the stairs, remaining close with his beloved daughter.

THE LAPERAL HOUSE

The Laperal house sticks out for more reasons than its ghosts. In 1898, the Treaty of Paris was signed. The treaty forced Spain to give the Philippines to the United States. The US governed for 48 years. During this time, many Americans settled there. The Laperal house is famously designed in the American Colonial style. This showed that the Filipino Laperal family had as much money and power as the Americans living there.

the nanny

Roberto Laperal

the little girl

CHAPTER 4

ENDLESS WANDERING

Sarah Winchester married into the family that made the Winchester rifle. This gun was popular all over the United States. Sarah and her husband William had a daughter. **Tragically**, their daughter died soon after she was born.

LEARN MORE HERE!

The Winchester house has beautiful grounds surrounding it.

More trouble followed. Sarah lost her father-in-law and her husband in the next year. She fell into a deep sadness.

One day, Sarah met with a **psychic** to try to contact her lost loved ones. Instead, the spirits of those killed by Winchester rifles came through. The psychic told Sarah she was cursed by these ghosts. They were responsible for the deaths of her loved ones! The psychic told

The first Winchester rifle was made in 1866.

Sarah that she was next. The only way she could live was to start an endless construction project.

So, Sarah moved to California and bought land. Construction on a house began in 1884. Sarah paid her builders extra to work day after day. There was no plan for the house. Nearly 600 rooms were built. But because the home was constantly remodeled, only 160 exist now.

Inside the house is a maze of rooms and dead ends. Hallways lead to nowhere. Rooms are plastered over. Doors open to brick walls or nothing at all. This was intentional. Sarah wanted to hide from the ghosts haunting her. They never caught up.

After Sarah died in 1922, construction stopped. People were fascinated with what was left. The mansion became an official California historical landmark. Visitors hear the sound of nails falling to the ground in the hallways. Lights turn on by themselves. In the basement, the ghost of one of the builders pushes his wheelbarrow back and forth. The house hung on to some ghosts long after the last hammer sounded.

Sarah Winchester had staircases built that led to nowhere.

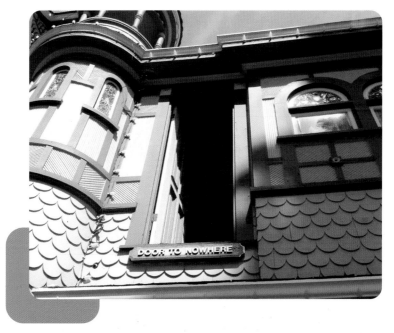

MAKING CONNECTIONS

TEXT-TO-SELF

Have you ever visited a haunted house before?
If so, did you have fun? If not, would you like to?

TEXT-TO-TEXT

Have you read any other books about hauntings
or ghosts? What did they have in common with
these stories?

TEXT-TO-WORLD

Do you think there are certain places in the
world that have more haunted homes than
others? Why or why not?

GLOSSARY

chamber — a room.

garrison — a place where soldiers stay.

mansion — a large home.

plaster — to use a pasty mixture that coats walls and ceilings. It hardens when it dries.

psychic — someone who can communicate with spirits.

torture — to cause very bad pain as a form of punishment.

tragedy — a horrible or unpleasant event that causes a lot of harm.

World War II — (1939-1945) a major war fought in Europe, Asia, and Africa. Great Britain, France, the United States, the Soviet Union, and their allies were on one side. Germany, Italy, Japan, and their allies were on the other.

INDEX

ONLINE RESOURCES

popbooksonline.com

Scan this code* and others like it while you read, or visit the website below to make this book pop!

popbooksonline.com/haunted-homes

*Scanning QR codes requires a web-enabled smart device with a QR code reader app and a camera.

HAUNTINGS

Books in This Series

Distributed in paperback by

North Star
EDITIONS

POP! IS A DIVISION OF ABDO
ABDOBOOKS.COM

ISBN: 978-1-64494-676-3

90000

9 781644 946763